GALE
CENGAGE Learning

Literature of Developing Nations for Students, Volume 1

Staff

Series Editors: Elizabeth Bellalouna, Michael L. LaBlanc, and Ira Mark Milne.

Contributing Editors: Elizabeth Bodenmiller, Reginald Carlton, Anne Marie Hacht, Jennifer Smith.

Managing Editor: Dwayne Hayes.

Research: Victoria B. Cariappa, *Research Team Manager.* Maureen Eremic, Barb McNeil, Cheryl Warnock, *Research Specialists.* Andy Malonis, *Technical Training Specialist.* Barbara Leevy, Tamara Nott, Tracie A. Richardson, Robert Whaley, *Research Associates.* Scott Floyd, Nicodemus Ford, Sarah Genik, Timothy Lehnerer, *Research Assistants.*

Permissions: Maria Franklin, *Permissions*

Manager. Margaret A. Chamberlain, Edna Hedblad, *Permissions Specialists.* Erin Bealmear, Shalice Shah-Caldwell, Sarah Tomasek, *Permissions Associates.* Debra Freitas, Julie Juengling, Mark Plaza, *Permissions Assistants.*

Manufacturing: Mary Beth Trimper, *Manager, Composition and Electronic Prepress.* Evi Seoud, *Assistant Manager, Composition Purchasing and Electronic Prepress.* Stacy Melson, *Buyer.*

Imaging and Multimedia Content Team: Randy Bassett, *Image Database Supervisor.* Robert Duncan, Dan Newell, *Imaging Specialists.* Pamela A. Reed, *Imaging Coordinator.* Dean Dauphinais, Robyn V. Young, *Senior Image Editors.* Kelly A. Quin, *Image Editor.*

Product Design Team: Kenn Zorn, *Product Design Manager.* Pamela A. E. Galbreath, *Senior Art Director.* Michael Logusz, *Graphic Artist.*

Library of Congress Cataloging-in-Publication Data

Literature of developing nations for students / Michael L. LaBlanc, Elizabeth Bellalouna, Ira Mark Milne, editors.

v.; cm.

Includes bibliographical references and index.

Contents: v. 1. A-L — v. 2. M-Z.

ISBN 0-7876-4928-7 (set: alk. paper) — ISBN 0-7876-4929-5 (vol. 1) — ISBN 0-7876-4930-9 (vol. 2)

1. Fiction—Stories, plots, *etc.* 2. Fiction—History and criticism. 3. Developing countries—Literatures

—History and criticism. [1. Fiction—Stories, plots, *etc.* 2. Fiction—History and criticism. 3. Developing countries—Literatures—History and criticism.] I. LaBlanc, Michael L. II. Bellalouna, Elizabeth. III. Milne, Ira Mark. IV. Title.
PN3326 .L58 2000
809'.891724—dc21
00-056023

Copyright Notice

Copyright © 2000
Gale Group, Inc.
27500 Drake Road
Farmington Hills, MI 48331-3535

ISBN 0-7876-4929-5

Printed in the United States of America.

10 9 8 7 6 5 4 3 2 1

I, Rigoberta Menchú: An Indian Woman in Guatemala

Rigoberta Menchú 1984

Introduction

When Menchú's autobiography was first published in 1984, it catapulted her and her story, describing the exploitation and mistreatment of her people, to the forefront of international attention. The book imbued her work in organizing the Guatemalan peasantry with added authority and credibility. The voice of the Guatemalan peasants, which had been heretofore silenced by government oppression, illiteracy, and linguistic barriers, was now available to the global public, and Menchú's narrative encompassed the story of oppressed people everywhere. Critics alleged that parts of Menchú's story were exaggerated or untrue, some even pursuing years of fieldwork to prove their allegations. Supporters have insisted that the verisimilitude of her story extends from the commonality of her experience with that of other Guatemalan peasants, in fact, most Guatemalan peasants. Menchú eloquently delineates the conflicts between ladinos and Indians, landowners and peasants, the government and the resistance, men and women, and change and tradition.

Author Biography

In this autobiography, Rigoberta Menchú details the two stages of her life: before political organizing, and after. Because she was born into a life of varied suffering and extreme poverty, and because hunger and crippling labor were constants, she was always conscious of the repercussions of Guatemalan politics in her personal life.

Every year of her childhood was divided between her home in the *Altiplano,* where Indians cultivated their own land and made every attempt to live as their ancestors had, and the coast, where the *fincas* were located. For most of each year, her family would leave the *Altiplano* and go down to the *fincas,* or plantations, on the coast, and endure inhumane work and living conditions picking cotton or coffee. Many children accompanied their families to the *fincas,* and many of the younger ones died of malnutrition or disease.

It is when Menchú becomes a worker in the *finca* at the age of eight that she experiences the true magnitude of the exploitation by the landowners. Indian workers always incurred debt at the plantation's cantina, pharmacy, and general store, so Menchú's family would sometimes leave the *finca* at the end of eight months with little or no money to show for their work. Simultaneously, what little land the Indians had managed to cultivate successfully in the mountains was constantly being seized by the government, or by landowners with government ties.

Menchú's community had always impressed upon her the importance of maintaining the ways of their ancestors, and they saw the encroachment of *ladino* as a direct threat to their way of life. Menchú saw, quite readily, the discrimination suffered by her people, and the divisive measures employed by the *ladino* society to keep the different Indian groups separate, so that the Indians, who were the majority population in Guatemala, could not unite and resist the discrimination and exploitation. Her growing awareness about this dire situation sparked her entry into activism, and she risked her life to organize the peasants against this abuse.

Menchú's father, Vincente Menchú, a leader in their Indian community, was also well aware of this exploitation, and worked most of his life to improve working and living conditions; he, his wife, and his son were brutally killed by the government for their activism. Menchú left Guatemala for a short period, when her own life was most in danger, but she ultimately returned to continue her resistance work. She was awarded the Nobel Peace Prize in 1992. She used some of the money accompanying the prize to establish a foundation in honor of her father, and continues to travel and write extensively, speaking out against social injustice. In 1998 she published a sequel to her autobiography, titled *Crossing Borders.*

Plot Summary

From the time she begins working on the *finca* at age eight, Menchú sees that the position of Indian workers is beyond grim. Workers make the long journey to the plantation by truck; because they are covered with a tarp, and not permitted to get out during any stops, the smell of human and animal excrement is unbearable. A large lean-to made of branches with one crude outdoor toilet is meant to serve four hundred or more workers. The landowners find various ways to cheat the workers, by changing quotas or charging exorbitant prices at the plantation cantina, where many workers would go to drink away their suffering. Landowners spray pesticides on the fields while workers are present; one of Menchú's friends dies as a result, one of many who is killed by pesticide poisoning.

One year, on the *finca,* her youngest brother dies, and her mother is faced with going into debt to bury him on plantation grounds, or waiting until they return to the *Altiplano*; she elects to go into debt and bury him right away, as Indian custom demands, and the other workers provide what they can to help Menchú's family. Menchú recalls, "Those fifteen days working on the *finca* was one of my earliest experiences and I remember it with enormous hatred. That hatred has stayed with me until today." When the family, who had been scattered among various *fincas*, reunites at their home in the *Altiplano,* the news of her brother's death is the greeting Menchú and her mother bring.

When she is almost thirteen, Menchú becomes a maid in Guatemala City, the capital. She works with another maid, Candelaria, an Indian who has become "ladinized," that is, she has learned Spanish and abandoned some of her Indian ways. Nonetheless, Cande, as she is called, is kind to Menchú and helps her learn her duties, and also shows Menchú how to stand up to the mistress, who is a petty, demanding woman. During her time as a maid, Menchú witnesses the full force and cruelty of *ladino* discrimination against Indians; Menchú sees that the dog is fed better than she, that Cande is given a bed while she must sleep on the floor. Fearful of losing her ties with her family, and unable to contain her anger at the way she is treated, Menchú leaves. When she returns home, she learns that her father has been imprisoned for resisting the government's takeover of Indian land. Given that illiterate Indians have virtually no recourse in the justice system, it takes a combination of superhuman effort and luck to get him out.

In 1967, Menchú's village in the *Altiplano* is "repressed" by the army for the first time. When land cultivated for years by Indians finally began to produce, landowners appeared, ransacked the village, and forced the Indians out. Government authorities, in collusion with the landowners, took advantage of the Indian's illiteracy by coaxing them to sign documents which the authorities claimed gave Indians the deed to the land. In reality, the documents stated that the Indians would be allowed to remain on the land for two years, after which they must move to another area. It is during these early conflicts with the landowners and the government that Menchú discovers the power of language, and the multiple ways that Indians are cheated, divided, and abused because of their illiteracy. She vows to learn Spanish, which she knows is, in many ways, a break with her community, since in learning Spanish, she will learn many other ways of *ladinos.* It is also at this time that the CUC is created—the Comité Unidad de Campesina, or the United Peasants Committee. Both Menchú and her family are active leaders of the CUC at different points in its history.

The government's next step is to disrupt the communal structure of Indian village life by giving each Indian family a parcel of land, too small to cultivate efficiently. The Indians resist, and combine their parcels into a common area, divided into cultivated land and living areas for all. Since Menchú's parents had long been the leaders of their community, they are elected to live in the center, with others surrounding them. The government's response to this resistance is to send in soldiers to break up the villages by force; the soldiers, some of them recruited Indians, engage in mass looting, murders, rape, and torture. Menchú's community decides to defend itself by placing booby-traps all around the village, and they are successful, even managing to capture one of the soldiers. In accordance with their respect for human life, they do not kill the solider, but impress upon him how wrong his actions are, and beseech him to tell his comrades the same. After this success, Menchú travels to nearby villages and organizes them in a similar way.

One of Menchú's earliest experiences with organizing was facilitating Bible study meetings in her community, which was largely Christian, thanks to the influence of Catholic Action, a religious organization started in 1945 to spread Catholic doctrine among the Indians. Menchú explains that Indians took to Catholicism readily because the Bible and Indian culture had many elements in common, such as veneration of ancestors, expression of thanks to a God, and the promise of a better afterlife for suffering endured on earth. Once she decides to learn Spanish in order to better organize the peasant population, Menchú receives most of her tutelage from sympathetic priests. She does recognize, however, that there are two Catholic churches in Guatemala: the church of hierarchy, which turns a blind eye to the Indians' plight, teaching Indians to be passive and accept "God's will," and the church of the poor, which actively joins the struggle, with priests and nuns risking their lives in the same way, for the same cause.

As Menchú and her family become more active in the CUC's resistance activities, they become wanted by the government. Menchú's younger brother is kidnapped and brutally tortured by the military, and her family is called to watch him and other prisoners be burned alive. If they refuse, they would be arrested as accomplices. After the death of her brother, Menchú's father, as part of a mass protest, occupies the Spanish embassy, where they are killed when troops set fire to the building. Menchú's mother is captured, raped, tortured, and left to die of exposure on a hilltop, her open wounds infected and suppurating. Her body is guarded by soldiers, to ensure that no one comes to save her or claim the body; they guard the corpse until it completely disintegrates.

Ultimately, Menchú renounces marriage and motherhood, for several reasons. Although she acknowledges that having children is natural, and that family planning is another abomination placed on Indians by the *ladino* society, she cannot bear the thought of bringing children into the world who will suffer as she has. Also, she knows that her work will be limited by having children, and while many men in the organizing movement are very enlightened about their common plight, that many are also trapped in the chauvinist ways of thinking which place men above women.

Forced to go into hiding after the death of her mother, Menchú barely avoids capture while hiding in a church. She works briefly for a group of nuns at a convent, until she learns that they are often visited by a member of the secret police. She escapes to Mexico with the help of non-peasant members of the resistance movement, and is reunited with her four sisters. She rejects the offer of European supporters to go to Europe, and returns to Guatemala, where she begins to work as an organizer for the Vincente Menchú Revolutionary Christians, a group formed in memory of her father, an unceasing activist and devout Christian.

Candelaria

Candelaria is the "ladinized" Indian maid with whom Menchú works in the city. Cande is unimpressed by the mistress' fits and threats, and stands up to her without hesitation. She even plans a small rebellion in the house, to annoy the mistress, but is thrown out when her plot is discovered. Cande refuses to sleep with the sons of the house, inciting more mistreatment from the mistress, but still, she is able to demand that the mistress give Menchú's father some money when he appears one day, penniless.

Petrona Chona

Doña. Petrona Chona is the "first dead body" Menchú had ever seen. She had been hacked to pieces by the landowner's bodyguard because she refused the landowner's son. She was married and had a small son, whose finger was chopped off during the attack.

Petrocinio Menchú Turn

Petrocinio Menchú Turn was Menchú's younger brother, who was kidnapped, tortured, and killed by the army for his organizing work. His family was called to witness his murder by the army; the army lined up all the prisoners, doused them with petrol, and lit them on fire as their families watched. He was Menchú's second brother to die.

Juana Menchú

A community leader alongside her husband, Juana Menchú was a woman of varied talents; in addition to running an ever-growing household in strict accordance with Indian customs, she was immensely knowledgeable about natural medicines, and her services as a healer and midwife called her away from home much of the time. Menchú admits that because of her patience and resourcefulness, her mother was the one "who coped with the big problems in our family." Also an activist in the peasant's struggle, she is ultimately captured by the military and tortured in unspeakable ways, and dies an agonizing death.

Rigoberta Menchú

Menchú describes herself as "shy, timid," during her younger years. She was her father's favorite, and her father's staunchest supporter, sympathizing with his need to drink to drown his overwhelming sorrows. As for her mother, she regrets not having taken the time to learn as much from her mother as she did from her father, particularly when, after the death of her mother, she notes that women bear most of the suffering of families, and know the most secrets. Perhaps due to the influence of her parents, who were leaders of the community and wholly Indian to the core, Menchú also becomes a leader in both the Christian and peasant organizations without sacrificing her Indian beliefs. She does, however, consciously decide not to be married or become a mother, identities which are integral to womanhood in the Indian culture; she decides, with difficulty, that her mission to work for social justice is one which cannot accommodate the challenges of motherhood. She is a tenacious and intelligent figure, able to learn Spanish without formal schooling, without being able to read or write. Her narration of her story is replete with an understanding of political struggle: why barriers exist between people, what fuels injustice and exploitation, what will precipitate change. She is astute enough to look at Catholicism critically, although she is a devout Christian, and select those elements of Christianity that will help her struggle and which will not. Her courage and unceasing stamina allow her to organize other villages on her own, to venture into the city at the age of twelve to work as maid, and to risk her life organizing all peasants, *ladino* and Indian, as a leader in the CUC.

Vincente Menchú

Orphaned as a teenager, Vincente Menchú is the driving force behind the village's resistance. In the army, he learned "a lot of bad things, but he also learned to be a man." He was often away from the house, petitioning government authorities, organizing workers, or imprisoned, but he was Menchú's favorite, and she his. He is killed while occupying the Spanish Embassy, when troops set fire to the building. He was very intent on teaching his children to fight, as he had been taught, and passes down the ideology of cultural pride and resistance.

The Mistress

The *ladino* who employs Menchú as a maid, the mistress is a symbolic representation of all *ladinos* who discriminate and oppress Indians. Her appallingly unfair treatment of Menchú is Menchú's wake-up call to the true nature of racist *ladinos.*

Themes

Community

The book contains detailed descriptions of Quiché Indian ceremonies, traditions, and customs, which Menchú gives in order to explain the profound sense of community which fuels Indian village and family life. The village is an extension of the family, and all previous generations are represented in the village through remembrances of ancestors and their ways.

Topics for Further Study

- Research ancient Mayan culture, with particular emphasis on respect for nature and family and rites of passage. Compare and contrast the salient elements of ancient Mayan culture and modern Quiché Indian culture. What has remained intact? What has evolved?

- Investigate the United States' involvement in Guatemalan politics and economy from 1960 to 1990, with emphasis on the U.S. anti-Communist policies of the Cold War. What were the effects of U.S. intervention on Indian land holdings and family structure?

- Trace the development of Menchú's feminist sensibility, and the way she acknowledges, confronts, preserves, and adapts traditional notions of family, motherhood, womanhood, and *machismo.*

- Analyze the structure and recurring themes of Menchú's story as testimony. Compare and contrast her testimony to African-American narratives, such as those of Frederick Douglass and Malcolm X. What themes of struggle and oppression, as well as triumph and resilience, are present in both narratives?

The ceremonies for childbirth, marriage, and death all emphasize the importance of community involvement. A pregnant woman is given all the comforts and attention that the village can afford, and the birth itself is one of the rare occasions when the village will kill an animal to celebrate. Indians engage in intricate ceremonies to ask the earth's permission before sowing and harvesting; it is considered blasphemous to abuse the land, when the earth is the mother and father of all that exists upon it. Marriage is undertaken only after an elaborate series of visits by the prospective groom and his parents to the bride's family; the bride makes the ultimate decision. Even after marriage, if the situation becomes untenable, the bride can leave her husband and his family and return to her village, where the community will care for her, feeding her out of a communal surplus which she, in turn, contributes to with her labor. For death rituals, the community, not the family of the dead, bears all the expenses of the burial. It is one of few occasions when flowers are cut, to be placed around the coffin. Before his death, an Indian will offer his secrets to one chosen person, and all of his advice and his recommendations to his family. Menchú says, "We can only love a person who eats what we eat," explaining that when encountering non-Indians, the willingness to accept Indian ways is a crucial sign of empathy.

One other significant aspect of all these rituals, which has developed since the appearance of the *ladino,* is the pact that all Indians make at certain milestones (birth, ten years of age, marriage) to uphold and maintain the ways of their ancestors and to "destroy the wicked lessons we were taught by [the White Man]," since "if they hadn't come, we would all be united, equal, and our children would not suffer." Even these century-old ceremonies have adapted to include not only an acknowledgment of the Indian's history, but a call to consciousness of the Indian's present situation at the hands of ladinos, and a promise to battle the forces which endeavor to corrupt Indian ways.

Language and Literacy

Menchú's community has an oral tradition through which they pass information about traditions and history from one generation to the next. Because of the variety of language spoken among the larger Indian population, however, Menchú finds that Indians cannot communicate with one another, despite their similar circumstances. Menchú's family is afraid that she will acquire other undesirable *ladino* traits if she learns Spanish, but *ladinos* have kept Indians from learning Spanish anyway, by keeping them out of their homes and schools. Menchú learns how disempowering it is not to be literate, particularly in Spanish, when her family is cheated into signing documents they did not understand, which ultimately left them landless. The chapter where Menchú describes her decision to learn Spanish to organize peasants more effectively is titled "Farewell to the Community: Rigoberta decides to learn Spanish." Her decision is based on the logic that "Since Spanish was a language which united us, why learn all the twenty-two languages in

Guatemala?…I learned Spanish out of necessity."

Natural World

Menchú refers to the earth as "the mother of man," because she "gives him food." Animals, water, and maize are considered pure and sacred, and are often invoked in prayer. Menchú also notes that "they" call the Indians polytheistic because they acknowledge the God of water, the earth, and the son, but she explains that all are expressions of the one God, "the heart of the sky." All life originates with this one God, and for that reason, Indians promise to respect all life, killing neither trees, plants nor animals without good cause or first asking permission to do so from the earth. Even when the Indians begin to organize the villages to protect themselves from the army, they ask the "Lord of the natural world, the one God," for permission "to use his creations of nature to defend" themselves. For this reason, the indiscriminate killing of people and animals by the army is still more shocking to the Indians.

When Catholic Action began to spread the Christian doctrine among the Indians in 1945, the Indians willingly accepted it as not a discrete religion, but another means through which to express their existing indigenous beliefs and practices, such as prayer. Menchú delineates the similarities between Catholicism and Indian beliefs: "it confirms our belief that, yes, there is a God, and yes, there is a father for all of us…we believe we have ancestors, and that these ancestors are important…the Bible talks about forefathers too… We drew a parallel [between Christ] and our king, Tecũn; Umãn, who was defeated and persecuted by the Spaniards." Later, Menchú finds that the Indians can use the Bible as a weapon in the struggle for social justice, observing that the Kingdom of God where all humans are equal should be created here on earth, despite some teachings of the Church that compel Indians to be passive and accept "God's will."

Migration and Dislocation

Movement and relocation are the two primary modes for Indian living conditions, since Indian families can only spend a third of the year cultivating their own land at home in the *Altiplano,* spending most of the year away at the *finca.* When traveling to the *finca,* Indians attempt to replicate a sense of home by bringing their animals, utensils, and other small possessions, although doing so makes the long journey by truck uncomfortable and sometimes unbearable. The dislocation is underscored by the fact that Indians are covered by a tarp while traveling, making it impossible to see the countryside they cross. Furthermore, when the government begins to force Indians off their own communally developed land and onto individual parcels or uncultivated land, it exacerbates the sense of dislocation by forbidding the use of basic natural resources that are critical to the Indians survival, such as trees. The Guatemalan Forestry

Commission begins to require advance permission for cutting down trees, and when permission is granted, charges the Indians exorbitantly for them, although corporations are seen freely cutting down hundreds of trees for business use.

Style

Setting

Menchú's story begins with the story of her parents, her orphaned father and her abandoned mother, who both matured under the same impoverished conditions as Menchú herself. In her narration, Menchú takes the reader from the dreadful conditions of the *finca* to the difficult but fulfilling communal life.

Point of View

The book is written in first person, from the point of view of Menchú, who has learned to speak Spanish through immersion. She is in her early twenties when she dictates her story to ethnographer Burgos-Debray, and she describes not only her life story, but the stories of her father and mother, other villages, and the evolution of the CUC (The United Peasants Committee).

Symbolism

There are two salient symbols which Menchú weaves through her narrative: maize and talk. Maize (corn) is the center of the Indian economy; they eat, sell, and feed their animals with maize. They hold elaborate ceremonies before the first yearly harvest of maize. Childbirth ceremonies reaffirm that humans are made of maize, and how the essence of humans can be found in maize. Maize is the life-blood of the Quiche Indian culture.

Talk is another important representation of Quiché culture; it is through talk, spoken language, that those near death pass on their recommendations and secrets, and it is through talk that young people and newlyweds reiterate their commitment to the community and its ways. It is the inability to talk to one another that keeps the different Indian ethnicities from uniting effectively against their common oppressors, the *ladino* landowners and government. When tortured by the army, Indians have their tongues cut or split, so they will not be able to talk of the atrocities they have suffered, or pass along warnings and true stories of brutality.

Literary Heritage

I, Rigoberta Menchú: An Indian Woman in Guatemala has a dual literary heritage, descending from ancient Mayan/Quiché Indian culture and shaped by modern Guatemalan social forces. As a spoken narrative which was transcribed and put into print by ethnographer Elizabeth Burgos-Debray, and translated into English by Ann Wright, Menchú's story was left virtually intact the way it was narrated. The act of telling her life story, replete with recommendations, explanations, as well as concealed information, is one of *testimonio,* a form common to Indian culture. Testimonio, or testimony, is, according to Zimmerman, "a culminating life act," and Menchú's testimonio is "like that of one who is going to die." In describing the funeral ceremonies in the Indian community, Menchú notes that before death, the dying will call his family to him and "tells them his secrets, and advises them how to act in life, towards the Indian community, and towards the *ladino.* That is, everything that is handed down through the generations to preserve Indian culture." Essentially, that is what the peasants struggle is as well: a persistent attempt to preserve Indian culture, their way of life, in the face of *ladino* encroachment. The purpose of Menchú's narration is not only to describe this struggle, but to be a part of it.

During times of crisis, Zimmerman notes that writers evolve new forms of expression, and in

Guatemala, this new form embraced the use of metonymy, using one entity to represent other things associated with it. Menchú acknowledges right away, on the first page, that her story "is the story of all poor Guatemalans." Although it seems impossible, her story is the story of all Guatemalans, not only through the use of metonymy, but accumulation. Just as the recommendations of the dying integrate the story of his life and the advice of all those who came before him, Menchú's story encompasses not only her family's life but the lives of all families like hers.

In *Teaching and Testimony,* Arata describes a "flexibility of expression" which was a "crucial part of Mayan resiliency," facilitating their survival through centuries of invasion, oppression, and hardship. Arata contends that this "ability to adapt without giving up what is most important provides a continuity through change," a statement which further clarifies how Menchú's people have managed to remain so consistent and true to the ways of their ancestors despite the relentless modernization going on around them. It is also true of the structure of her story, which is fluid, moving seamlessly between a chronological narration of events to detailed descriptions of Indian customs. Burgos-Debray explains that she left all the parts of Menchú's story in the order that it was told, despite worries that it might be confusing or boring to the reader; her editorial decision preserved the fluid, flexible structure of Menchú's narrative which places it so firmly not only in her native oral tradition, but her cultural imperatives.

Historical Context

A Thirty-five Year Civil War

When Guatemala's economy changed from an agrarian economy to an trade economy based on coffee in the late 1800s, the government needed more and more land on which to grow this lucrative cash crop. To satisfy its need for land, the government employed a strategy known as "land grabs," whereby arable land was forcibly taken from Indian villages and used to grow coffee and other cash crops. Because coffee was labor intensive to process, the government began to pressure Indian communities to work on plantations, as Pratt explains, by "passing a 'vagrancy law' requiring all landless peasants to work for at least 150 days per year for either the *fincas* or the state." This law, in conjunction with the military's takeover of Indian land (thereby rendering Indians "landless" in the eyes of the law), is the reason why Menchú's family and so many others had to migrate to the coast for most of every year to work on the *fincas*.

A new government came into power in 1944, beginning a period known as the "Ten Years of Spring," with Arbenz as president. Labor and land laws were modified to favor peasants' rights, land was taken from corporations and redistributed back to peasants. Unfortunately for the peasants, the largest corporate landowner was United Fruit Company, a U.S.-owned conglomerate, who cried foul and "Communism" back in the States, which was experiencing the McCarthy anti-Communist juggernaut; United Fruit had a monopoly on fruit exports from Guatemala, and it "stood to lose 400,000 acres," in the land redistribution, according to Pratt. The Arbenz government was overthrown in a U.S.-backed military coup in 1954, part of the United States' worldwide anti-Communism campaign, and was replaced by a military dictatorship.

Organizers such as Menchú and her family members, and Indians in general, because of their communal ways and organizing work, were labeled as Communists and became government targets nearly overnight. It was during the period of authoritarian rule following Arbenz' administration that the "land grabs" were in full force; peasant lands were once again forcibly reappropriated and peasant resistance crushed. The guerrilla movement developed in response to the government's brutal tactics, in tandem with a groundswell of grassroots organizing, such as literacy campaigns, farming cooperatives, and health initiatives for the poor. The government responded to guerrilla reprisals by organizing death squads, such as the notorious "La Mano Blanco," or the White Hand. During a peaceful occupation of the Spanish Embassy, against the protests of the Spanish ambassador, the army set fire to the building, killing all but one protester, including Menchú's father.

An irony is that *the finca* system actually brought groups of Indians into contact, a gathering which would have been difficult otherwise, given the remoteness of most Indian villages. Indians from different groups were able to meet and compare experiences and, eventually, communicate and organize. Perhaps one of the largest triumphs of the resistance was the coalition established between *ladino* peasants and Indians, manifested during the strike of over 75,000 workers in 1980. It was a coalition which could only develop when racist, classist, and linguistic barriers were finally minimized.

Critical Overview

Menchú's autobiography has been attacked by critics for being an "inauthentic" text. Critics charge that there has been "interference" from editor and ethnographer Burgos-Debray, who interviewed Menchú, or that Menchú herself exaggerated or fabricated parts of her story to make it more dramatic. One of Menchú's earliest and most vocal critics, Dinesh D'Souza, former editor of the conservative college paper the *Dartmouth Review* and author of *Illiberal Education,* questioned the veracity of Menchú's status as an impoverished victim of centuries-old discrimination, exploited by corrupt landowners. He offers her vocabulary, her later travels, and her conversion to Catholicism as dubious proof of her victimization. David Stoll, a professor at Middlebury College in Vermont, conducted years of fieldwork in Guatemala and claims to have found people whose recollections of events described by Menchú differ greatly from hers. He asserts that the truth about Guatemalan politics at that time was far less extreme and polarized than Menchú suggests, and that "the people" were more ambivalent about which side— the guerrillas or the government—to believe.

Advocates of Menchú's counter that the structure and content of Menchú's story are both accurate and typical of the period during which Menchú matures and tells her story. Zimmerman argues that in a "crisis period" such as that of the

1960s-1980s in Guatemala, that writers create "new forms representing new perspectives…each… straining to express…the social whole," such as the form created in Menchú's autobiography. Menchú explains herself, on the first page, that her story is the story of all poor Guatemalans: "My personal experience is the reality of a whole people." Menchú's supporters contend that it is not the sheer veracity of her facts that determines the value of her story in a political-social context, but that the verisimilitude of the Guatemalan peasant experience is revealed, made accessible, and honored.

Zimmerman, and others, note that Menchú does not use metaphor to develop her descriptions, but metonymy. Metonymy is a literary device which uses the name of one entity to represent the idea of all other entities associated with it. In reference to Menchú's story, that means Menchú's story, and her name, invoke the story and names of all other poor peasants. Her use of the pronoun "I," Zimmerman reasons, "is imbedded and absolutely tied to a 'we.'" In this sense, Menchú's supporters are not acknowledging and excusing falsehoods in her story, but asserting that an inconsistency or contradiction in her story does not render it an inauthentic or unimportant text, because in the balance, it tells the true story of poor Guatemalan peasants who were, in fact, exploited, tortured, and killed.

Another critical aspect of Menchú's story is the method through which it came to print. This book requires an unusual definition of authorship; is the author the person who tells the story, or the one who writes it down? Burgos-Debray, the editor of Menchú's story, assures the reader in her introduction that the narrative that Menchú relayed orally was not altered in the slightest. This book has a special status as literature, spoken narrative, autobiography, and historical text, since it is the true-life story of Rigoberta Menchú, a Quiché Indian woman. Menchú did not actually put pen to paper to write the book; it is the unabridged transcription of her story, which she told in Spanish, to ethnographer Elisabeth Burgos-Debray over the period of a week. (An ethnographer, simply put, is someone who studies other cultures.) Burgos-Debray recorded Menchú's story, transcribed it, organized it, and put the words in print, in Spanish. That book was then translated into English by Ann Wright. The exact words and the flow of the story are Rigoberta Menchú's, but others put her story into book form.

As the book is essentially the printed version of an oral narration, theorists have placed Menchú's autobiography in the genre of "testimonio," or testimony, an oral form prevalent in Quiché culture, and a literary form common in Latin American literature, whether printed or oral.

What Do I Read Next?

- *Crossing Borders* is Menchú's 1998 sequel to her autobiography *I, Rigoberta Menchú: An Indian Woman in Guatemala.* In it she details her continuing work and struggles after receiving the Nobel Peace Prize in 1992.

- *Rigoberta Menchú Turn: Champion of Human Rights* is a biography of Menchú appropriate for secondary-school readers.

- *Guatemalan Women Speak,* is a collection of translated statements from *ladino* and Indian women on a broad range of topics including "Earning a Living," "Being Indian," and "Fighting Back."

- *Rigoberta Menchú and the Story of*

All Poor Guatemalans, by David Stoll, is decried by supporters of Menchú as a conservative attack on Menchú's purpose in telling her story, and praised by others as an enlightening analysis of inconsistencies in Menchú's story.

- *Teaching and Testimony: Rigoberta Menchú and the North American Classroom,* a collection of essays written by college professors and teachers about the use of *I, Rigoberta Menchú: An Indian Woman in Guatemala* in their classroom, offering a comprehensive analysis of historical context, literary form, and critical theory.

- *Kaffir Boy: The True Story of a Black Youth's Coming of Age in Apartheid South Africa* is a powerful autobiography of a young man confronting the horrors of discrimination, abject poverty, and police terrorizing, and, against all odds, becoming a tennis player who eventually wins a scholarship to an American university.

Sources

Arata, Luis O., "The Testimonial of Rigoberta Menchú in a Native Tradition," in *Teaching and Testimony: Rigoberta Menchú and the North American Classroom,* edited by Allen Carrey Webb and Stephen Benz, SUNY Press, pp. 82-83.

Bell-Villada, Gene H., "Why Dinesh D'Souza Has It In for Rigoberta Menchú," in *Teaching and Testimony: Rigoberta Menchú and the North American Classroom,* edited by Allen Carrey Webb and Stephen Benz, SUNY Press, pp. 50-51.

Beverly, John, "The Margin at the Center: On *testimonio* (Testimonial Narrative)," in *De/Colonizing the Subject: The Politics of Gender in Women's Autobiography,* edited by Sidonie Smith and Julia Watson, University of Minnesota Press, 1992, p. 94.

Carby, Hazel, *Reconstructing Womanhood: The Emergence of the Afro-American Woman Novelist,* Oxford University Press, New York, 1987, p. 74.

Moneyhun, Clyde, "Not Just Plain English: Teaching Critical Reading with *I, Rigoberta Menchú,*" in *Teaching and Testimony: Rigoberta Menchú and the North American Classroom,* edited by Allen Carrey Webb and Stephen Benz, SUNY Press, pp. 238-39.

Pratt, Mary Louise, *"Me llamo Rigoberta Menchú: Autoethnography and the Recoding of Citizenship,"* in *Teaching and Testimony: Rigoberta Menchú and the North American Classroom,* edited by Allen Carrey Webb and Stephen Benz, SUNY Press, pp. 60-65.

Rochelson, Meri-Jane, "'This Is My Testimony': Rigoberta Menchú in a Class on Oral History," in *Teaching and Testimony: Rigoberta Menchú and the North American Classroom,* edited by Allen Carrey Webb and Stephen Benz, SUNY Press, p. 249.

Zimmerman, Marc, "Resistance Literature, Testimonio, and Postmodernism in Guatemala," in *Literature and Resistance in Guatemala: Textual Modes and Cultural Politics from El Senor Presidente to Rigoberta Menchú,* Center for International Studies of Ohio University, 1995, pp. 25-26 (Vol. I), 54-55 (Vol. 2).

Further Reading

hooks, bell, *Feminist Theory: From Margin to Center,* South End Press, 1984.

> A series of easily accessible essays addressing the topic of feminist political and personal action, in practical terms, from solidarity with other women to the nature of work, relationships with men, education, and struggle, among others.

Gómez-Quiñones, Juan, *Chicano Politics: Reality and Promise 1940-1990,* University of New Mexico Press, 1990.

> A political history of Mexico and in the United States, delineated along chronological and ideological lines, clarifies similarities and differences in the conditions of laborers and their fight for social equality and justice.

Roediger, David R., *The Wages of Whiteness: Race and the Making of the American Working Class,* Verso, 1991.

> A dense but thought-provoking investigation into the process of racial identity formation, and the effects of this racial identification on the size, strength, unity, structure, and progress of the American

working class and labor movement. Sheds additional light on why the barriers between *ladinos* and Indians remained intact for so long, so tenaciously.